She Hands Me the Razor

SHE HANDS ME THE RAZOR

POEMS BY

RICHARD KRAWIEC

Press 53
Winston-Salem

Press 53
PO Box 30314
Winston-Salem, NC 27130

First Edition

A Tom Lombardo Poetry Selection

Cover design by Kevin Morgan Watson

Cover art, "Rub-a-dub-dub," Copyright © 2011 by Samantha Tran

Printed on acid-free paper

ISBN 978-1-935708-36-0

To the Washington Street Writers group,
for over two decades of friendship, laughter
and heated arguments over poetry.

And to David, Danny, and Sylvia,
who have brought joy and love to my life.

We appear to be at the mercy
But then again it may be we have not yet come
To the mercy, that we will never arrive at the mercy.

—Denis Johnson

CONTENTS

Introduction by Tom Lombardo   xi

I. Love

Young Love   3
She Hands Me the Razor   5
Spring Suite   6
Handling Lies   9
Worship   10
After the Lie   11
Breakdown   12
God's Face   14
Don't Worry   17
Things To Do When You Lose a Child   19
Even the Dog Is Depressed   20
A Father Fights With His Son To Get Ready for School   21
Judging the Worth   22
Evidence   23
The Free World   24
The Mockingbird Sings Me Back   26
Diverging Paths   27
Love Turns   28

II. Loss

Usher   31
At 16   33
Blink   35
The Other Pittsburgh   36
Failure: To Protect   37
There Will Always Be a Father   39

Waiting To Be Beaten   41
Neighbors   42
Broke   43
Unemployment   44
At the Borders   45
The Eater of Smiles   47

III. Redemption

Rip Current   51
New Advent   53
Pressing and Yearning   54
The Installation of Art   56
Logo   58
Autumn Love   60
The Waiting Room   61
Prognosis   63
Ventilator   65
After Death   66
First Advent Without   67
Approaching Grace   69

INTRODUCTION
BY TOM LOMBARDO

If the title of this collection leads you to expect edgy, sharp poems, you will not be disappointed, but you must not be surprised by the flip side of the title's implication, that this collection is permeated by a persistent, soft undercurrent of vulnerability.

When a woman hands you her razor, she must trust you to do something very private, whether the ultimate purpose is pain or pleasure. When a woman hands a poet her razor, all bets are off. The poet can take that razor into the imagination and return it coated with something red, something white, or something black. Whatever happens, as poet Richard Krawiec writes,

> it is always a matter of finding
> another's boundaries
> one's own limits

Mr. Krawiec's collection, *She Hands Me the Razor,* pushes up against, and sometimes explodes through, the boundaries of both his and his readers' shared truths. This tense and tender collection delves deeply into love, loss, and redemption, which could be the subtitles for each of our lives.

In one poem, poor young people live on love and bread and arias. In another, a marriage shatters due to a cone of psychosis. In yet another, the effects of that breakup and insanity show up in disruptive ways in the unfortunate victims, the children. One critical boundary broken is the line the poet must cross to begin recovery, and that moment becomes a metaphor in Krawiec's poem of a mockingbird whose song reveals the world's secret. And the poet turns, just like a sonnet turns, and life

> adjusts
> its top hat, scarf, then strolls
> jauntily out the door

Of course, it's not that simple. There are complications and much more to explore in the poet's "true/unblinking/mirror" held up not to himself but to you, the reader.

Enjoy the view.

Tom Lombardo
Poetry Series Editor

I. Love

YOUNG LOVE

we never knew
how impoverished
we were, living
on a futon
in a micro room
blanket-shaded
in roach-plagued Boston
we had coffee,
bread, vegetables
in the crisper
warm arms
arias of love
which wavered
through the sirens
of foot-shuffle night
our bodies
taut as bowstrings
harmonized
above the clank
and gutter
of morning
each day's sunlight
was brilliant
clouds and rain
a reprise
we failed to see
the peeling paint
awed by the flicker-
sprinkle of stars
beyond the window
the tangle and fold
of shadows

on the sheets,
our laughter
pushed back
expanded the walls
our love a run
of rolled 7s
luck we never
thought
would run out

SHE HANDS ME THE RAZOR

when I ask
she hands me the razor
trust or faith I don't know
where to begin to stroke
upward   downward
I press the three whip-thin
blades against her skin
how much pressure
does she need   do I want
it is always a matter of finding
another's boundaries
one's own limits
I pull slowly
across the arched muscle of her calf
the stretched tightness of her thigh
a few wisps of black hair escape
I press harder feel that catch
which halts my breath in mid exhaust
no rose blooms so I return
to the world of breathing
slower now I scrape off the lather
with mincing strokes reveal
each dimple freckle curve
consider the flesh
like Michelangelo
where to daub stroke edge
how to reveal   the many
smooth faces of God

SPRING SUITE

I.
there's something Egyptian
about the way the blossoms
bracelet the plum branches
a sifting jangle of floral rings
that gleam their way
from shoulder to wrist

the teasing hint of skin
flickers   the wind-slinked
arabesques seduce
the open pink lips
of petals glisten

II.
sharp   overwhelming
wind-snapped forsythia
blossoms burst forth
one after another and another
sunlight petaled
a bright scatter
rich grasping yellow
keening
against the hard, blue sky

III.
salt tang in the rich, musty delta

the slow vibration
of the thick-vined crescent

on the rippled flats,
beads of dew spread
burst into tributaries,

the hills beyond rise,
fall, seething with heat

a melodious laugh
a face with smeared lips
diaphanous hair wind-tousled

Handling Lies

what do you do
when her eyes sparkle
and she dances
side to side in glee
when she hugs kisses
and strokes you on arrival
her pretty mouth wide
in a loose smile
and the lies fog out
small wisps of ground
cover she insists

she is not really
untruthful the clouds
only interpretations
fudging a bit
don't worry   don't
look down
though the mist
has risen
to your knees
and everything below
is dissolving
she tells you
you're not really
falling

WORSHIP

we light the candle
in an upstairs room
read Bible verses
on 'love' 'forgiveness'
sing hymns to the power
of faith and healing
share a communion
of wine and crackers
as broken as we feel

in attempting
to heal
the torn sinews
of the past
we see
for the first time
our perishable flesh
hints of wattles
lines and wrinkles
the past chiseling
towards the future

we reach to embrace
what remains
kiss stroke hold
worship
the stark light
of the declining sun
our adoration
the dark purple
petals wild irises
of the soul still
furling forth

AFTER THE LIE

…she promises repentance with eager kisses, grasping fingers which clutch and fold the cloth of his sleeves, as if holding the fabric tightly will pull his body back so it will once again fill his clothing.

Because he is shrinking; his cells have boarded the bullet train to nanoland. She watches his dungarees pool at her feet, lifts the empty shirt, shakes it.

The microscope beckons from her end table in the back bedroom. It sits, layered with dust, unused since the last time. She knows she should grab it, snap the illumination bulb on, and search for him, draw him up in a pipette, mount him on a slide, culture his cells, revive him. Raise him to maturity.

But through the frosted glass of her front window the horizon is streaked, mango and rose light glows behind the blue-rimmed cirrus clouds. She releases his shirt and steps forward into the dawn, into the welcoming coo of mourning doves.

BREAKDOWN

like the aftermath of violent tides
piled leaves debris the street
your parents called again
again I told them
nothing
what do they wish
to hear from me

that your older brother
armed with a dictionary
ordered you to comply
with his words of assault

younger brother pinned
your arms as he arched and sliced
into your body

father got you
drunk in a hotel room in Mexico

mother bruised
you to silence with egg beaters
hair brushes and wooden spoons

now they enforce silence
with flowers cards claims of love
and the repeated emphasis
on the suffering you cause
them
by curling on a bed
in the Psychiatric Ward
of the State Hospital

safely hidden
inside a code
of Oz   tornadoes
and Bizzaro cartoons
that bring you messages
from the Virgin and her angels

in this world you are always
three years old and killing
your children
watching yourself
be tossed raggedly
down the staircase
you believe in your fault
you can never be
sorry enough

so you construct a grid
of global conspiracy
to make your violators
heroes who saved you
by leaving clues
to what they'd done

the leaves are thick
I tell your mother
and as each one breaks down
the piles seem larger   more
impenetrable

we are your mother tells me
having a nice autumn

God's Face

the sky is a gray fur
so close and dense the skin
of heaven remains unseen
the blurred circle of the moon
resides behind
like the empty socket
of a removed eye

the sharp stones of the driveway
press through my slippers
I lift the damp newspaper
scan today's headline tragedy
some figure skater bruised
on the knee by her rival
I drop the paper
into the thin black stream
flowing down the gutter

the tortured souls I love
wait anxiously for me at the window
three faces pressed to the glass
three sets of dim sockets no
visible eyes their need is granite
weighting my shoulders their silence
desperate pleas which pull me back
to the jaundiced interior
of our leaky-roofed house

how can I save them

my oldest son destroys
his demons in preschool fights
tantrums thrown when recalcitrant
toys taunt him by not bending
to his will   he pounds his head
to punish himself for his mother's illness
punches friends so he will not have to
punch her   his face is so torn
by anguish I fear it will scar
him worse than any knife
his only escape comes
from the pacifying tube
where the Mighty Morphin
Power Rangers teach him
there is evil to fight then leave
him frustrated to find the enemy
in his life has no face

on the verge of language
my youngest boy screams
each time he is touched
by this unknown woman
his mother   my wife
perhaps he knows
the vision she revealed to me
two hours past midnight
she saw him in the crib
saw her hand reaching
saw the delicate eggshell
shatter of his cracked skull

he spends his days stuck
like Velcro to my chest
hands hooked into my shoulders
a small solid presence
around which I scramble
breakfast   talk on the phone
shower and shave

and my wife   my wife
that assortment of nervous tics
evasive eyes psychotic
blips and accusations
a shuffle-gaited collection
of human fragments
held together by the loose bag
of her skin *I've lost*
my self there is nothing
there beneath the medication

Oh You Lord whose face
I imagine in this terminal
sky   feral and blind
to human possibility
do You wonder
why I doubt my own
ability to persevere

is Your vision contented
or am I misguided like Job
do I confuse the cross
for the cave   heaven for hell
perseverance for penance

Don't Worry

when she says she's afraid
she might kill
her baby
when she says she's worried
she could kill
her baby
when she says she thinks
about giving him
an overdose
when she imagines the headline
mom murders sitter
and child
when she says the reason why
this year is significant
is this is the year
he dies

don't remember
how she shook a toddler
so hard its head whipped
back and forth
or punched bruises
on your arms
or told stories
of her own mother
            slapping her face
            smashing her brother's head
            driving her car into the son
                    who misbehaved

it's organic
this illness
not the result
of environment
thoughts are random
illusions she surely
wouldn't act upon
they have drugs
amazing drugs
surely don't worry for
your
child

when she says
she knows
the secret   she will
kill him
when she tells you
the jump rope
would make an excellent weapon

THINGS TO DO WHEN YOU LOSE A CHILD

smell the mold
remember his downy face
cry on the sidewalk
refuse to move

sit by the phone
unplug the phone
chug wine
stare out the window

call in sick
write a poem
throw it away
spit in the barrel

get stoned
walk on water
slice off foreskins
pluck out an eye

Even the Dog Is Depressed

She mopes the day through this dusty house. The rain-drenched yard holds no allure. She must be pushed and dragged by the collar to the fenced-in back where instead of racing along the wire fence, scurrying through dense briars in search of game, she stands against the gate and bark-begs to be returned inside, where she cowers as the father grabs his adolescent son by the shirt front. Cups his left palm over the boy's mouth, and commands his child to shut up and listen, stop yelling and screaming, stop accusing his father of unfairness for criticizing the boy for poking his younger brother in the arm with a pen as part of the game the boy decided they must play. Just listen, the father screams, his voice stair-stepping louder than his son's, listen, first, please.

It is at this moment that the mother stalks through the room, cutting random swaths out of this scene with scissors which gleam like teeth in the night; her own eyes turbaned with a blindfold; her own mouth sputtering shards of confusion, as if she were spit-sowing seeds into a field already tangled, impassable with vines and weeds. Her words fall like dung, steaming heaps which cover the floor; she leaves, never to be seen again. That night.

And the youngest child, tears dried like clear ink on his cheeks, stands on the furthest threshold, the one leading to his bedroom, breathing through his mouth. He clutches a book and watches, silent. Nobody sees him.

Not even the dog.

A FATHER FIGHTS WITH HIS CHILD
TO GET READY FOR SCHOOL

His excuses fall
like the ripped paper snow
in an amateur theatrical,
a cheap illusion
whose drifting glitter
momentarily obscures
the costumed players,
the soldierly father,
the sobbing child
who now breaks
into silence
at the threat
of abandonment;

appeased,
the father spackles
over his anger
with a thin, patch
of reason, seeks
to explain, to reassure
himself that he hasn't
really
flayed open his son
with the blade of his words.

Judging the Worth

another 5AM wake-up call
from the child who has learned
the joy of song before language
he alternates high then low *doos* then *lats*
the melody brooklike   a wander without refrain
his child's scat lacks the edge of sex
and sorrow adults impose on expression
do-lat-deet-da-duuuh-lo-lo-lo-loooooow

outside it is all mist and fog
the yellow notes of streetlights
diffuse like brilliant words that have lost
the structure of their argument
I watch a small tornado rise
from the exhaust of my neighbor's car
my son hunches into my chest
it toooowl he says   and I agree
it is cold but his breath warms
my shoulder his chest protects my own
he burrows his arms between us
one hand pops free his fingers slide
over his thumb as if testing fabric
the weight and weave judging the worth
of this life   he throws his head up laughs
his teeth small and bright as stars
the firmament his face radiates

around us hidden in the dark branches
of the pines and hardwoods   birds
chorus a greeting; the cacophony
of their song edges towards clarity
if I can only stand still long enough
to listen

EVIDENCE

the Christmas fir leans
against the last budding branch
of the sheared stump of the apple tree

tawny blades of grass
stiff with white frost fail to contain
the clumped spears of the wild onions

like mica ice flashes
star points from the green leaves
of the wind-shaken mulberry bush

before a small wooden chair
a pink corn cob stripped of kernels
evidence something survives

THE FREE WORLD

My son keeps on rocking
in the free world with Neil
Young   he races past the couch
slams into the closet door
spins and runs across the living
room to dive onto the futon
he stands to display a series
of convulsive jerks   as if
electric currents attack
his limbs in random patterns
the uncontrolled   arrhythmic
spasms only a white   five-year-old
boy could conceive
his release is my salvation

last night he told me he never
wanted to sleep again   he barricaded
his room with light   the three-bulb
overhead   the carousel horse lamp
the beams of four flashlights   he is sick
of shadows   wants no more dreams
of monsters who lurk outside
his vision   unseen   undefined
as intangible as his mother's illness
which he cannot touch or identify
and so finds impossible to banish

His brother toddles into the room   bouncing
his butt to the beat in the air
he yells *hey*   thrusts his arms
high and falls hard onto the rug
he smiles and beckons with his hands

how many invitations do I need
I push aside the texts on incest
and depression rise shake my own
butt in the air   yell *hey* slam
into the wall   race back and forth
across the room grip and haul
both boys upward   pull them close
kiss their faces with fierce insistence

the shades are up   the lights on
anyone passing might look in
it matters that they see us
that they know

we whirl about the room
three as one dancing singing
rocking our own way
to a world we would like
once again
to be free

THE MOCKINGBIRD SINGS ME BACK

to the glass-toxic streets
of East Durham; barred
windows, a rancid coal stove,
the time-thickening heat
when another mocking bird

sang me away
from the bloated dead mice,
grease-coated walls, bride
immobilized
by filth and distance
wailing on the mattress;

sang me to wonder
so that I stood
on the termite-crumbling porch
gape-mouthed, and let the sweat
course through the soot
on my face, overwhelmed

that a bird knew
the world's secret
every voice can be ours
can pry open a shelled heart,
and no voice can speak
to a heart deafened by lament

DIVERGING PATHS

from different rooms
the scolding rip of packing tape,
soft click of prayer beads

one son pounds drums
the other shuffles pages of a book

outside, the mated cardinals
still perch together
and sing

LOVE TURNS

milk will not uncurdle,
river upwards into the carton

seeds can't climb through soil
and leap back into pods

the phantom limb remains
an empty, folded pant leg

for a while you smile, mouth
those same three words

while your heart adjusts
its top hat, scarf, then strolls
jauntily out the door

II. Loss

USHER

In the pool hall no one laughed
at his misshapenness;
the elongated head, brown, sloe-eyes,
body stooped and bent
as if his bones were pipe cleaners

John Hasomeris,
the name itself a drift
of sound, breath escaping
in a leak.

And though we wore our costumes
of leather and denim, wavered,
drug-fogged, beside the brushed felt tables,
no one smirked at John as he neatly hung
his cardigan sweater on a ripped stool,
then leaned over to stroke the cue,
send the balls rattling like bones
towards the black maw of the pockets.

In the perpetual midnight
of the dim-bulbed room,
he was just one more outcast
seeking asylum, though we didn't know
the assassin coursing in his veins
was less forgiving than the cocaine
and heroin shooting through ours.

Three days into summer my 15th year
the newspaper named his death.
Leukemia. He was the first classmate
who would never come back.
I settled before the TV set
to watch the Jetsons, Beany and Cecil,
shake my head. I didn't know how
to call my friends and talk.

With working parents we had no one
to guide us into dark jackets, lead us
to the funeral home where we might
have helped him leak to the next world,
helped ourselves escape this one.

Four decades later, I don my black suit,
light the incense, kneel before
the rusted Celtic cross.
I whisper the mantra of his name,
Hasomeris... Hasomeris...

At 16

the snowstorm brought a great mercy
of cancelled school, parents required
to leave for work   outside

my bedroom window the white gleam
of sledding laughter, bundles
of children sliding the snow-dazzled street

I'd always loved that cold-blind
downhill rush, the stinging muffle
of icy wind on my face

but instead I dug for the locked box
buried beneath the pile of mold-
scented clothing in my closet

I bolted the door against
my eager brothers and sister
hung blankets over the windows

to block out the least smidgen of light
dry-swallowed the tab of LSD
cranked Jimi Hendrix loud on the stereo

the rush jolted upwards from my gut
through my chest, nailed my eyes
to an unfocused openness

so the flowers dancing across the ceiling
blurred with the echoing voices of Jimi
and his wah-wahing guitar

for eight hours, through Zeppelin,
Floyd, and Zappa the parade of hallucinations
exploded in synchronic flow

across the dripping swirls
of the ceiling, walls, the breathing rug
and laughing voices stabbing my ears

until the slow wear-down
left me spent, gasping, bent
over the strychnine pain in my stomach

ensconced in my self-inflicted tomb
I listened to the crystal laughter
of the lives outside

BLINK

a small child
bundled
like a blue marshmallow
unloads
before the school
flips
a wave at the wagon-taxi
battered
with decades of dents

barking
the pit bull cargoed inside
lunges
at the staring children
who don't shuffle, or even
blink
their glassy eyes

The Other Pittsburgh

is not steel
or coal or the potato wedge
face of a European pap pap
it is not Carnegie
or football or Mellon
it's only union
is the wedding of violence
when Joey smashes David
in the face for sleeping
with men he didn't
rob   and Tonya weeps
as she straps the children
of the man who whipped
a scar on her face
it is the sideways appraisal
of the 10-year-old boy
who will open you
with a knife
as easily as he would slide
down his zipper to reveal
destiny to his sister
or brother or whoever needs
to learn this is his
city too

FAILURE: TO PROTECT

Like a music-drugged rock star
Tyler's head swivels
a figure eight
above the Braille machine
while he bangs out a story
of abandonment and acceptance

Monique's pink and downy
scalp glows over the paper
her lips pucker an inch above
she reads like a lover
bestowing a kiss
to the tale of herself
as an alien freeing an alien dog

Zach's fingers puzzle
each letter of Braille
he types, struggling
to get the spelling right
so he can share his premature
birth, detached retinas

The Braille Writer spits
out sheets which say
DaVonte's character bursts
into ashes, overloaded
with homework, his parents
die of stroke, blinded
by the letters of their assignments

Her frizzed afro, held in a T
by a wound elastic, quivers
as Diamond writes of that incredible gift
a visit to Food Lion, the ritual
to pack her clothing for the trip

When I ask Brandon
if his character, Princess Poach,
might open her parasol
and float into his life
he laughs at me, "That's too much
imagination." I am the one
who seems to be lacking.

How dare I whine to myself
about friends distanced
by divorce and ennui,
about lovers and sons
and their gnat-irritations?
How dare I inflate
into torment the small
discomforts of my day?

When
Cassidy smiles
despite her noseless face
Kimberly giggles,
the gray discs of her eyes
darting side to side,
Tavish, head lined
with an incision scar
from ear to ear across his dome
stutters with joy because
he learned how
to dribble a basketball?

There Will Always Be a Father

Gary Gilmore, just before he was executed by firing squad

an apparition fades
into the doorway at night
some nights   not many
merely an outline of limbs and torso
cropped shell of a head
settled into slumped shoulders
and the boy always clutches
his blanket in silence   waits
for an arrival which never comes

each morning car exhaust
drifts from the blue mist
streaked above the dirt driveway
slithers beneath the crooked kitchen
door   pools at the Formica table
where a solo coffee cup glows
with streaks of dried brown liquid
and morning sunlight

that familiar man
with a nose like a dented tuber
who smiles and nods without talking
tucks a paper napkin into the collar
of his starched white shirt
snuffles and snorts through mashed potatoes
and meatloaf   then stands to blow his nose
on a soiled handkerchief he fondles
into the back pocket of his chinos
as he walks away   again   to work

the water pipe sizzles
as each boy clicks his Bic
lighter   sucks in a deep betrayal
of smoke   overhead the floor complains
in the cellar room teenagers clench their breaths
but it is only the house settling
boards pulling apart unseen   and all
guffaw clouds into laughter
except for the one who sucks hard
on the pipe to hide his disappointment

and there will always be an executioner
knife or gun or bludgeon or needle
the sharp shining blade of a guillotine
a baggie full of rainbow pills
empty vodka bottles tipped across countless counters
lubricious girls who spread themselves
upon rutted mattresses on the floor
money waded in his pocket   bank account
funds   stocks   vacation homes   BMW
mistresses   herpes   divorce lawyers
cancers and heart disease
and the late nights alone when he stares

no more at the ocean   moonlight
chopping a long wavering flame
from horizon to shore
but instead gazes at the memory
of an outlined figure   apparition
which never steps over the threshold
of the always open door

Waiting To Be Beaten

an old rug hangs
from the wires
before the Royal Inn
a stucco wound
masquerading as comfort
for the perpetual hopeless
men of bag-sagged eyes
and four-day beards
women bound
with barbed wire
and rose tattoos
on wine-
flaccid thighs
even the rip
of cocaine
or a bloodied fist
fails to move them
beyond this

dust-laden hairball bed
to a streaked window
where the rising sun
still glistens yellow
then white

NEIGHBORS

before the bungalow
two police cruisers grumble
one officer stands on wet asphalt
leans towards the second car's
open window

my neighbor's father mother
pace the edge of the driveway
shake gray-haired heads
mouths furrowing deep
like trench-turned clay

at the side door
my neighbor's wife slouches
arms folded across her chest
her body trembles   head ticks
in a slow disbelieving arc

the standing officer calls
over his shoulder looking nowhere
that it's just an argument
a sudden angry squawk erupts

on their front lawn
beak to beak two mocking
birds rise in an upright flutter-
fight wings beating the air
above the quiet circle
of wilted impatiens

BROKE

turning away from

the scrofulous rat
running
inside the basement

the banded spiders
nesting
beneath the box spring

the winged ants
swarming
the foundation

the unpaid bills
blank
checkbook ledger

the children
crying
the wife
frowning

the true
unblinking
mirror

UNEMPLOYMENT

a row of cold houses
light like a foot-crushed
blossom of purslane
so small and yellow
it fails to pass
the whining window panes

even the small corners
of these front stoops
huddle in darkness

somewhere a dog barks
certainly a lover must moan
blue screens flare
a drainage ditch glows

on some corner
yesterday's debris
sparkles in the effluvial night

softly I breathe
my own breath fog
inhale the thousand effervescent
suns in the bluing sky

AT THE BORDERS

the woman in dancer's black
stretch top   skin-sleek
slacks draws a cigarette from the sea
green box of Newports

she doesn't have to pace
through this Borders
where single men
Armenian? Korean? Latino?
a verge of suspects
tic-tac-toe the cafe

simply carrying her iced
and cream-topped coffee
sliding a cigarette from fingers
to mouth is enough

to send heads ducking
to notebooks cell phones
any pretense of purpose
besides loneliness

why do we connect
if not to mountain-mist
the obvious
we are all alone
and dying

Rilke had his panther
sleek and muscular
padding behind steel bars
while men watched from without

now men sit imprisoned
behind wooden chair slats
while she stalks
across the dark interior
into the sunlight
where they no longer belong

The Eater of Smiles

folds the golden wedge
to his mouth with a cup-
ped hand, like a mime
donning a mask, everything
changes—the stippled skin
shows between his red lips,
hiding the teeth that bite
and grind the soft, lemon-
tart flesh attached
to that shining skin
which his lips close
moistly over

III. Redemption

Rip Current

to the surfer whose face
I don't remember
more a failure
of character than observation
I can't believe
the curl I caught
twenty feet from shore
ripped me seaward
a thousand feet out
to a doldrum surface
the size of a battlefield
framed by the crashing froth
of twelve-foot swells
all the information
I'd memorized—stroke
at an angle towards shore
or swim parallel
out of the current failed
when the ocean refused
to behave like Wikipedia
and my arms would only move
like the 58-year-old tools
they are, and not
the arms of memory
after five minutes of no
movement save backwards
drift with the outgoing tide
I scanned the steamed mist
horizon listened to the cross-hatched
sea sizzle like the burning
bodies of soldiers entrenched
and doused with kerosene

fearful of losing
the one thing that might
keep me alive
I clutched tighter
to the smiling sea turtles
of my kiddie boogie board
and floated seaward
beneath the acid rays
of the sun

like Michael the Archangel
you were suddenly there
winging forward
over the deep water surf
I grasped the black cord
dangling from the back of your board
stroked, true, and kicked
a little, but mostly let myself
be led like a child
holding hands across the divide
of the terrifying intersection
of tide and current
I'm sorry I failed
to earn your grace
by remembering anything
about you and maybe
in a quantum universe
I am paying for my sins
by gulping burning draughts
of salt thick water
as I swirl to the bottom
you never let me know

New Advent

you stood sunlit
before the cathedral
jewel-red beret,
jaunty smile, hip
tipped in welcome.

I didn't know
there'd be glitter
shining softly
in your hair, silk
as it brushed my lips;

or that the glisten
and gleam of your eyes
would be candle bright
in the prayer room
outside the church
where the journal
before the statue
of suffering Mary
held strangers'
scribbles,
wails of despair,
hopelessness, falling short.

In the spontaneous
moment when we turned
to gather each other,
arms grasping,
hungry as mouths,
pulled our eager bodies
into that swirl
of breathless loss,

I didn't know
where we'd been
or where we were
going.

PRESSING AND YEARNING

You stood on the stool
so you could reach down
cradle my face up to yours;
we slow-danced to Van Morrison
'Have I told you lately
that I love you?'

You above, pressing down,
me yearning, always this
pressing and yearning.

Once I closed your eyes
circled you slowly, touched
gently with my tongue the places
you wouldn't anticipate
I lifted you to the bed,
pressed into your yearning,
you tossed your hair
a storm of disarray
then kissed and laughed
your way down my body.
I stroked and glided
your arms, stomach, legs

after we tucked our feet
beneath the covers,
drank wine, pecked
tortellini, salad,
each others' lips.

What is this we have,
where nothing is more loving
than anything else—a kiss,
a phone call, the flash of eyes
at the market, feather-slip
of hand on   back
lips on neck?

They say the spirit yearns
to God, or the universe, longs
to join the cosmic symphony.

When we press and yearn
we are already there,
absorbing, dispersing, singing
What better home
could we possibly find?

The Installation of Art

On the muddy pond
iridescent globes shimmer,
focus the declining sun
into reflecting flames
glow through
the circular reflections,
sphere kissing sphere.
Figure eights you say,
infinity I think, and grasp
your warm hand
feel the heat pinged
with a hint of cold;
we are too old to pretend
we have forever.

Angled bamboo stalks
rise from the water,
circle the grassy banks,
less fence than erratic
guideposts. But the globes
are tethered, unable
to escape or maneuver
through, find a path,
limited to slow, solitary drifts,
a reflective shine,
those magnificent
tongues of light—
two lovers
pressed together
in the center.

When we settle
on the ground
the sun dazzles your smile,
glitters your gray hair to blonde.
I push you back onto the warm
grass, just to hear the flame
of your laughter.
My face declines
to yours, arms encircle;
our light reflects inside
each other, two strong,
unwavering pulses,
guiding us all the way
to the sunset.

legs twine on the logo
of the Quality Inn, ribbon
limbs of gold that flow
in an imaginary breeze
rising from the solid green
background—a welcome
we can't resist

we use our AARP discounts
to splurge on a king-size
bed, and after I warn
the high school partiers
away—*I want you to have fun*
but not against my door—
I turn to the curve
you insinuate on the sheets

we snake-slither each other
writhe arms, legs, slide
skin over skin, tongues
and lips flutter, our soft
throaty laughter steams louder,
erupts into moans
and the teenagers
fall silent, disperse

outside in the fog-drizzle
the drunken laughter bobbles
slowly down the balcony
the shuffle-pad of footfalls
patters away

were you to perch
atop the motel sign
would you see
the peaked and shadowed
background of sheets,
framing a flow and twine
of living limbs, as one more
logo beckoning
hope in the night?

AUTUMN LOVE

on the dogwood
five red seeds dangle
from each broken star
of open, orange husk

the silk-feathered discs
of the butterfly bush
burst from their dried
and curling pods

a sour mash of apples
rotting in the high grass
fails to dissuade
the wren from singing

and you
whose eyes and smile
slide open within
the folds and wrinkles
of your face
like dayspring
coruscating through
the swaying pines

sow seeds
against the undeniable
cold flurries
of coming Winter

The Waiting Room

not double hospital gowns
rumpled large as samurai robes
nor forced laughter stretched smile
nods of reassurance

can hide how diminished she seems
shrunken like an aged child
by fear of the scalpel
and anesthesia's ability
to render thoughts
down to essence of smoke

every surgery threatens
a sunken barricade of stitches
the open seam in a cemetery

in the cafeteria's atrium
green-shaded lights reflect
on the inner glass
dew spackles
the solarium windows
a grass-sparse courtyard
studded with trees
and benches waits
uninhabited
in the morning's gruel
of sunlight

fear removes all makeup
glares to light loose skin
lines and moles
wrinkled hands
hanging pouches
witness reflect

our train is not chugging
out on a shiny track
but lurching on rusted rails
back to the station
we tumbled into each other
outside the club car
while searching for coffee
something to force us
awake

the track is loose
with missing spikes
the tunnel much closer
than we want to believe

I pull you close
and we do the one thing not allowed
the only thing left us
we dance in the waiting room
to songs of our own making

PROGNOSIS

this is the season of decay
mold and mushrooms sprout
through damp spongy leaves
the stench of wet rot
shivers
in the lightless woods
a roost of crows shriek
repeating outrage
one buzzard stumble-glides
down a deep ravine
disappears

on the dusk-smudged roadway
a deer thrashes settles
hind legs   hips demolished
an SUV angles off road
in tire-mudded grass   a white-
haired woman hunches
wrinkled hands clutch
a shaking face
I accelerate

from atop a dim bureau
the candlelight snake-flickers
my lover's eyes prism dust
I gore myself on her
an elephant attempting
to recant illness with lust
fingers grasp thighs   calves
skin patches and folds
the underpinning core
of muscle

my body jitters
demon wisps strop
the folds of my face chest
urgent and imperative
I drive forward
until sweat-sheened
spent

in the night
as dark as clotted blood
an owl's kill-excited coo
I pull the blanket-
shroud above
my head breathe
deflate still
awake

Ventilator

final holdout
I order the ventilator
removed

shutting down life support
losing more than her

it's time   I say   taking all her time   away

AFTER DEATH

the roses lower their heads
and there is nothing
you can do to stop
it   the leaves wilt
turn brittle
water grows stale and murky
no one can revive
no one can heal
grief
solace is soft
colors and scents
to gloss the bloody edges
pain recedes
because we grow weary
of crying
the wound scabs
the scar
never heals
years later a flash
of recalled gesture
smile touch
arrhythmia
clutches your breath
you throw out
the old bouquet for a new array
of diversion
and pretend to go on
undamaged

First Advent Without

there is nothing I can give you
not the soft whispers
of rain on a skylight,
nor the first lovely rush of heat
flowing into a cold room,

no rich bitter smells of wood smoke,
coffee, or the sweet milky scent
of a baby nursing

nothing to be heard,
no urgent harmonies of Bulgarian choirs,
foot-shuffle bop, or smiling scat-song,
nor the mournful lilt of a Celtic carol
whose smoke floats over the soft, flicker
of blue flames in the fire

I can offer no arms to encircle you,
no lips to nestle in the soft, yielding skin
of your throat, no gentle fingers
to caress your face, breasts, thighs....

all I can do is dance alone,
whirl and spin,
a dervish before my beloved,
my mouth, open, my love
my heart, my soul, a plea,
my love, my ecstasy ,
a pulse, a flow, my love,
my love, my joy, my love,
my spin-fevered body, a prayer,
collapse

there is nothing I can give you
this Christmas but the hope you will be
outside my window in the star-jeweled sky,
your face will feel my reaching hands
touch you, cradle you, draw you home.

Approaching Grace

a woman wearing a towel
shawl over a long dress
stands in the rush of tide
beating a bodhran
her body chants
from foot to foot
the white caps crash her hem

across the flagellant water
a crimson sun rises
above the mast of a shrimp trawler,
burns through the heliotrope haze,
the woman chants, beats, sways
her offered prayers lost
in the guttural glissade
of the sand-crunching waves

the woman I love arches
a sun salutation
her mermaid hair flows
wild tangles in the breeze
like the sea oats that shiver
their seed heads on the crest
of the weed-protected dune

along the porch railings
tourists peep out
tentative as snails
housewives in bathrobes
men in gym shorts and T-shirts
they smile shyly at me
in my paisley boxers

a Japanese mystic
claims the ocean contains
every thought that ever existed
the priestesses of Sangora
baptize with this wisdom
on the coasts of South Africa
I approach grace by watching

the feral curl of white froth,
rising sun, chanting woman
the red infusion of morning light
on my lover's already glowing face

ACKNOWLEDGMENTS

Some of these poems have been previously published in *sou'wester*, *many mountains moving*, *Artful Dodge*, *Connotations*, *Red-Headed Stepchild*, *Wild Goose Poetry Review*, *Helicon Nine*, *Off the Coast*, *Bear Mountain Review*, *The Write Place*, *Raleigh News & Observer*, *Luck: An Anthology*, *Living in Storms*, *Mamas and Papas anthology*, *Main Street Rag*, and *Where I Am—the NC Poet Laureate blog*.

RICHARD KRAWIEC has published two novels, a collection of stories, four plays, and a chapbook. He has won fellowships from the National Endowment for the Arts, the Pennsylvania Arts Council, and the North Carolina Arts Council (twice). His poems and stories appear in *Sou'wester, many mountains moving, Shenandoah, Witness, West Branch, North Carolina Literary Review, Florida Review, Cream City Review,* and dozens of other magazines. His feature articles have won national and regional awards. He teaches online at UNC Chapel Hill, where he won the 2009 Excellence in Teaching Award. He is the founder of Jacar Press, a Community Active Literary Publisher.

Cover artist **SAMANTHA TRAN** graduated from the University of Texas at Austin with a degree in Sociology and currently works for Dell, Inc. as a software specialist. She picked up photography as a hobby about two years ago and hasn't looked back since.

"I enjoy taking pictures of things that make people look at life the way I see it, or at least from my perspective," she says. "I also enjoy doing self-portraiture, and while that sounds horribly narcissistic, it's actually very cathartic to put yourself out there in photos to be critiqued and judged. It can also be easier than regular portraiture in that I don't have to try and communicate to anyone what I see in my mind's eye.

"For 'Rub-A-Dub-Dub,' I really liked the light in that bathroom, the way it bounced around the bathtub from the privacy glass above. I like photos with an open-ended story to them. Nobody knows what the girl in the tub looks like, or why she is there. It's open to interpretation. I think that always makes for a good photo."

Samantha is actively building her portfolio with plans to start her own photography business. To see more of Samantha's photography, visit www.flickr.com/photos/samanntran.

CPSIA information can be obtained at www.ICGtesting.com
Printed in the USA
BVOW021433170213

313425BV00001B/7/P